!NSPiRE

BREANNA STEWART

BY LEIGH LEWIS

AMICUS LEARNING

Inspire is published by
Amicus Learning, an imprint of Amicus
P.O. Box 227
Mankato, MN 56002
www.amicuspublishing.us

Editor: Ana Brauer
Series Designer: Kathleen Petelinsek
Book Designer and Photo Researcher: Emily Dietz

Library of Congress Cataloging-in-Publication Data
Names: Lewis, Leigh, author.
Title: Breanna Stewart / by Leigh Lewis.
Description: Mankato, MN : Amicus Learning, 2026. | Series: Inspire | Includes bibliographical references and index. | Audience: Ages 5–9 | Audience: Grades 2–3 | Summary: "Learn about basketball star Breanna Stewart and her accomplishments with the WNBA in an engaging profile packed with photos and fact-filled text suitable for young readers. Includes table of contents, glossary, further resources, and index"—Provided by publisher.
Identifiers: LCCN 2024044101 (print) | LCCN 2024044102 (ebook) | ISBN 9798892005159 (library binding) | ISBN 9798892005692 (paperback) | ISBN 9798892006231 (ebook)
Subjects: LCSH: Stewart, Breanna, 1994—Juvenile literature. | Women basketball players—United States—Biography—Juvenile literature.
Classification: LCC GV884.S74 L48 2026 (print) | LCC GV884.S74 (ebook) | DDC 796.323092 [B]—dc23/eng/20241118
LC record available at https://lccn.loc.gov/2024044101
LC ebook record available at https://lccn.loc.gov/2024044102

Photo Credits: Associated Press/Bill Shettle, 8, Hans Pennink, 7, Zach Bolinger, 10–11; Getty Images/Carmen Mandato, 20, Dylan Buell, 9, Elsa, 16–17, Gregory Shamus, 15, Mitchell Leff, cover, Sam Hodde, 4, Scott Taetsch, 18–19, Steph Chambers, 12, Tim Clayton - Corbis, 14; Shutterstock/grey_and, 6

Printed in India

Table of Contents

Stewart's nickname is "Stewie."

Basketball Star

Breanna Stewart guards the other player. She steals the ball. She runs down the court. She shoots. Swish!

Stewart is an American professional basketball player. She plays for the New York Liberty.

Around the Block

Bounce. Bounce. Bounce. Stewart's ball hits the sidewalk over and over. As a kid in Syracuse, New York, she ran four laps every day. She dribbled a basketball as she went. Left hand, right hand, spinning, between the legs!

SPECIAL TALENT

Stewie can juggle basketballs.

Stewart practiced hard when she was young. Her work paid off!

Stewart scored more than
2,000 points during high school.

Slam Dunk

In high school, Stewart dunked in a game. She jumped up high. Her hands were above the rim. She slammed the ball down. She scored. This was her first career dunk. The crowd went wild!

LONG ARMS

Stewie is 6 ft 4 in (1.93 m) tall. Her **wingspan** is 7 ft 1 in (2.2 m). Her long arms help her block and **rebound**.

College Star

Stewart went to the University of Connecticut. She graduated in 2016. Each year, her team came in first place in the finals. She is the only player ever to be named Most Outstanding Player all four years.

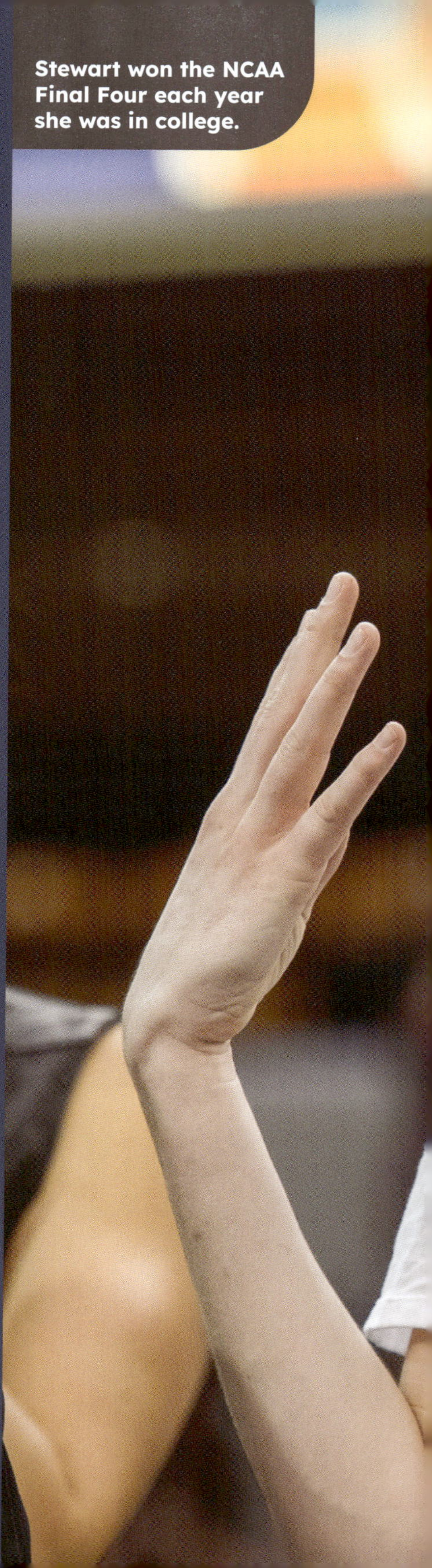

Stewart won the NCAA Final Four each year she was in college.

2016 NCAA WOMEN'S BASKETBALL
NATIONAL
CHAMPIONS
NCAA
WOMEN'S
FINAL FOUR

Stewart played for the Seattle Storm from 2016 until 2022.

Going Pro

Stewart went **pro** in 2016. She joined the WNBA (Women's National Basketball Association). There was a **draft**. The Seattle Storm picked Stewart first. She won Most Valuable Player (MVP) in 2018 and 2023. In 2023, she started playing for the New York Liberty.

DID YOU KNOW?
Stewie also played for teams in China, Russia, and Turkey.

Team USA

Stewart played for Team USA in the 2016 Rio Olympics. Her team came in first. She played at the 2020 Tokyo Olympics. They won again! In the 2024 Paris Olympics, the US beat France by one point. Stewart has three gold medals!

DID YOU KNOW?
At 21, Stewie was the youngest player on the US Women's Olympic team in 2016.

Stewart poses with her gold medal after the 2024 Paris Olympics.

Stewart and her wife have two children, Ruby and Theo (pictured).

Family

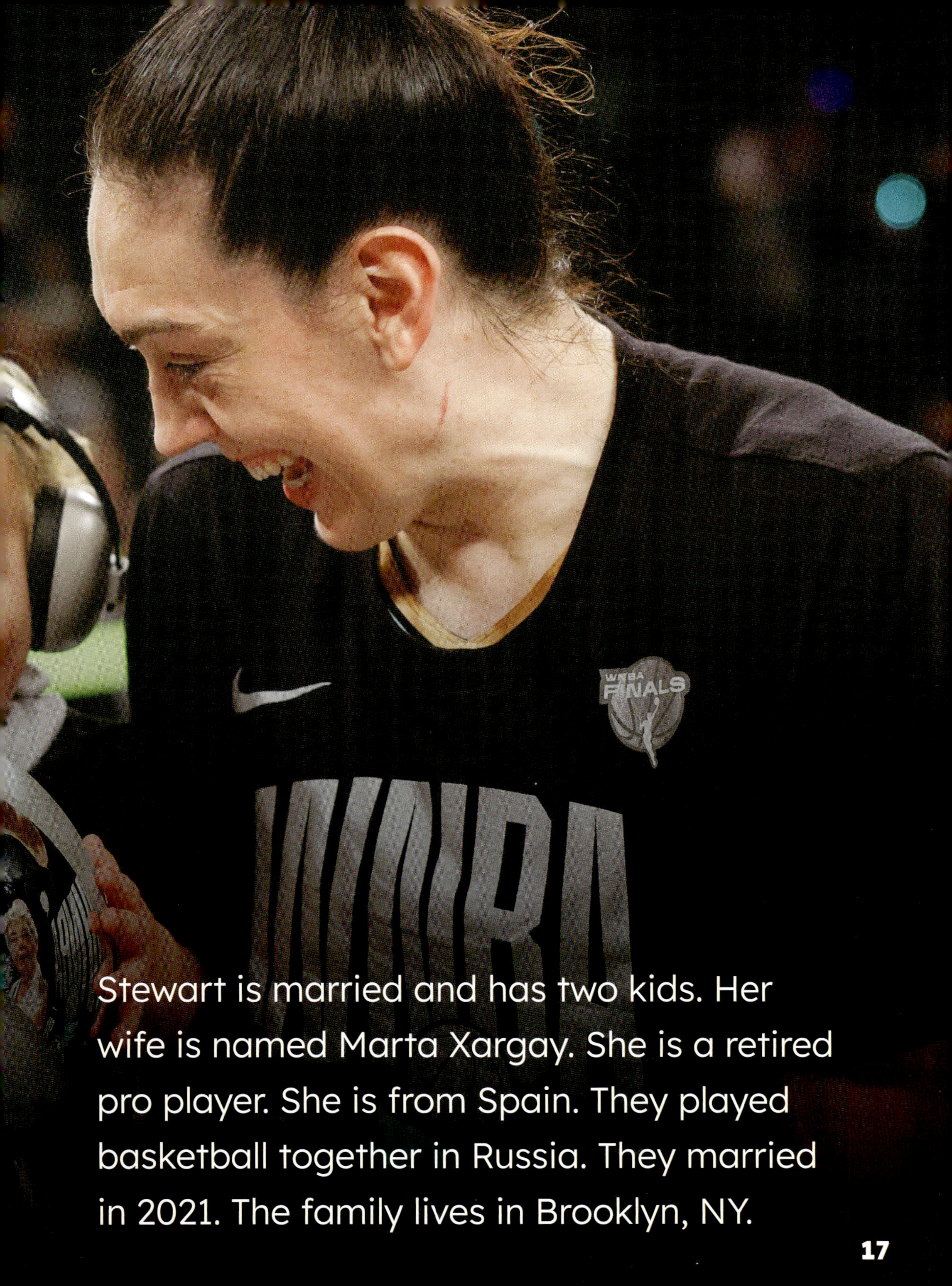

Stewart is married and has two kids. Her wife is named Marta Xargay. She is a retired pro player. She is from Spain. They played basketball together in Russia. They married in 2021. The family lives in Brooklyn, NY.

Speaking Up

Stewart uses her popularity to help others. She stands up for Black Lives Matter, the LGBTQ+ community, and women's rights. She believes working as a team is the best way forward.

Stewart often takes selfies with fans after games.

Unrivaled's first game was on January 17, 2025. Stewart played against her co-founder Napheesa Collier.

A New Game

In January 2025, Stewart co-founded a new league. It is called **Unrivaled**. It lets pro women's basketball players earn money during the offseason. Three players play per side. Games are played on a smaller court.

SUPER STATS

BREANNA MACKENZIE STEWART

Nickname: Stewie

Birthday: August 27, 1994

Hometown: North Syracuse, New York

Position: Forward

Current Team: New York Liberty

AWARDS

NCAA Champion: 2013–2016

NCAA Most Outstanding Player in the Tournament: 2013–2016

Final Four's Most Outstanding Player: 2013–2016

6-Time WNBA All-Star: 2017, 2018, 2021, 2022, 2023, 2024

Olympic Gold Medalist: 2016, 2020, 2024

Only person ever to win the Naismith Trophy 4 times

WNBA MVP: 2018, 2023

GLOSSARY

draft A process where teams take turns picking new players.

pro A professional sports player who is paid to play.

rebound Getting the ball back after someone has missed a shot.

unrivaled Having no competition, being the best.

wingspan The distance between a person's fingertips.

READ MORE

Chandler, Matt. **Breanna Stewart.** North Mankato, MN: Capstone Press, 2022.

Ford, Jeanne Marie. **Breanna Stewart.** Lake Elmo, MN: Focus Readers, 2022.

Labrecque, Ellen. **The Story of the WNBA.** Mankato, MN: The Child's World, 2020.

ON THE WEB

Official Website of Breanna Stewart
https://breannastewart.com

USA Basketball: Breanna Stewart
https://www.usab.com/players/breanna-stewart

INDEX

About the Author

Leigh Lewis is a children's author who loves her three kids, traveling, pickleball, and telling stories. She has lived in the US, Russia, Japan, England, Greece, and Turkey. Check out her books at leighlewisbooks.com.